The Lower Salt River flows through the Tonto National Forest at the northeastern edge of the Phoenix metropolitan area, referred to locally as The Valley of The Sun. This fertile floodplain, and the high ground around it, provides a home for scores of bird species, deer, bighorn sheep, big cats, and the Salt River wild horses--magnificent animals, descended from horses that carried the Conquistadores, and hauled supplies and people from east to west as this country was explored and settled. Today, they are living symbols of the principals of freedom upon which our nation was built.

The Salt River is about 200 miles long, but the relatively short 20-mile section of river that these horses call home lies between the Stewart Mountain Dam and the Granite Reef Dam. The herd is comprised of family groups called bands. Composition of a band will vary from one young stallion and mare awaiting their first foal to bands of a dozen or more with a lead stallion and a harem of mares, one of which has earned the title of lead mare who, as in most human households, keeps thing organized and running smoothly. The larger bands often contain a second, subordinate stallion--a lieutenant to help with security and overwatch. He is the first line of defense, meeting all threats head-on and giving the lead stallion time to move the band to safety. All band members take part in band security and protection of the young.

The herd's migration throughout this area varies with the seasons, which dictate what forage is available and where to find it, as well as breeding and foaling times. They seem to have a well-organized system in place which has served them well for 400 years or so.

The Salts have adapted well to this sometimes harsh environment and what it offers for sustenance to become a robust, resilient herd which has, so far, survived the encroachment of humans. They take little from the land, and the land, in turn, benefits by their being here--beyond merely providing plenty of organic fertilizer, from which both plants and birds benefit. Grazing the forests removes the understory, reducing the hazard of wildfire along the river. They feed on the reeds at the water's edge, keeping them at bay; and on the eel grass that grows thick in the river. All in seasonal rotation to maintain a year-round supply of food.

 "Snorkeling"--submerging their entire face in the river to graze on the eel grass--is an adaptation unique to the Salts. Youngsters who haven't mastered this usually wait for Mom to come up with a mouthful and mooch a meal from her.

Wild horses can get by on only three hours of REM sleep. Group members take turns dozing throughout the day while other band members keep watch--a particularly useful system when living in a forested area, rather than in the wide open expanses occupied by their cousins in Utah, Nevada, Wyoming and elsewhere in the West. They don't have the advanage of being able to see danger coming while it's still a long way off, so one or more in each band comprising the herd are always watching, keenly aware of changes in their surroundings

During the many hours I've spent watching these magnificent animals, I am always amazed by their sense of family, and their rules--etiquette, hierarchies, protocols and boundaries--which are, for the most part, respectfully observed by bands while interacting with one another in peaceful coexistence.

Equally amazing is how suddenly the peace can be disturbed by their response to breeches of those rules: Lead Mares or Stallions might chastise a band member for moving too slowly, or simply for being in their way. A Lead Stallion will vehemently defend his band against all interlopers wanting to claim any of his mares or offspring for their own. A mare might surprise a stallion by exercising her right to vigorously refuse his unwanted advances with bites and kicks. Groups of bachelors spar and tussle for the purpose of establishing their credentials in the band, practicing for those times in the future when it will no longer be a game. I once watched the interaction between two bachelors, one of which obviously had a "touch of the imp" that day. He began to purposefully annoy his fellow bachelor by gently nipping his neck and pulling on his mane. I watched as the patience of the "annoyee" wore thin until a full-blown tussle broke out. The "imp" knew it was coming, apparently craving it to break up the boredom of the moment, and his friend didn't disappoint him. It was just like a scene that plays out daily between siblings in households across America.

While the skirmishes and flare-ups of "horse drama" are spectacular, the times I find most soothing are the quiet peaceful stretches watching the more subtle nuances of band behavior. A nuzzle between band members that could be nothing other than a display of affection. A tender moment between a massive stallion and a youngster he has sired. A family simply enjoying each other's company--finding pleasure in the simplicity of a life of freedom.

Then there are those expressive eyes. When I am allowed to share their space, there is always a pair of those eyes on me. With only a stare and subtle cues of body language, these intuitive, insightful creatures have managed, at one time or another, to convey to me their curiosity, uncertainty, amusement, their trust or their lack of it, even their acceptance of my presence--the unspoken deal being that if I show them the same respect they extend to each other, they will return the favor in kind. I have not broken that deal with them, and they have rewarded me for it.

At first I dismissed these experiences as my imaginings. But it has happened again and again as I've come to recognize familiar faces and bands, and see recognition in their eyes. The reward is palpable. I leave them with a refreshed spirit, a restored soul and a renewed faith in the God that made them and guided them to this place. They provide me with a much-needed respite from a world working so hard at diminishing my faith in humankind.

One day a mare, grazing in the forest, watched me photographing the band and approached me to resume grazing quite nearby. I'd repeatedly move back to a safe distance--about 40 feet or so--and each time she would look up with a "where are you going" look on her face, and again move closer. Now, as touching as it is for such a beautiful, though wild, animal to demonstrate such trust and, apparently, her preference for being close to me, I know that to desensitize these horses to humans would put them in danger of being seen as a nuissance or a danger to the next family of picnickers they approached. This would eventually lead to their removal, which is unacceptable and completely avoidable. The possible danger to ME is obvious--it comes when a curious horse is spooked from behind by any sudden commotion, or if a stallion with none of this mare's trust sees me as a threat. So, knowing it's best for both of us, I reluctantly send them away with a shuffle of my feet or the squeeze of a water bottle, and a "thanks for the privilege."

It would be hard for me to imagine the Salt River without wild horses. I've come to value the time I'm able to spend among them; and I've come to realize that they are not mindless, soul-less creatures that are just taking up space. They're smart enough to utilize the meager resources available to sustain themselves every day; and they still make time to play, exercise, relax and socialize. They feel pain. They express love and affection, and morn the loss of a friend or family member. And it is my opinion, based on first-hand observations, that they're better at all of this than many humans. They ask so little of us other than respect and the freedom to share with us this beautiful, quiet corner of the world; and in return, they give so much to anyone willing to keep the unspoken deal they offer us--to anyone who is able to see the value of the gift.

In 2015, through the efforts of the Salt River Wild Horse Management Group, the Forest Service cancelled a roundup of the horses for removal, sale and/or slaughter. These American icons, living on our public land, belong to the American public--each and every one of us. And the SRWHMG's volunteers work hard to ensure that each horse born on the river has the opportunity to live out its life on the river. They've fixed miles of fencing to keep them as safe as possible from traffic through the area. They've offered a safe and economically feasible solution to on-range population management that is more humane than rounding up herds and storing them in holding pens until they're sold or slaughtered--which is what is happening to herds all across the West, at great expense to the taxpayers. Yes, us. And the only hope these symbols of freedom have is for the American people to be their voice because they have none of their own. Let your legislators know--by calling them, through social media, and by supporting the SRWHMG and the American Wild Horse Campaign--that the round-up and slaughter of wild horses is unacceptable.

We ALL lose if these magnificent animals are taken from us. They deserve better, and it will take all of us to keep them Wild & Free.

For over a year, the author has been photographing wild horses along the Salt River for the SRWHMG. An Arizona resident since 1972, he currently lives with his wife and daughter in Chandler, Arizona.